Skeleton, Skin and Joy

poems

Charles Atkinson

Finishing Line Press
Georgetown, Kentucky

Skeleton, Skin and Joy

Copyright © 2017 by Charles Atkinson
ISBN 978-1-63534-222-2 First Edition
All rights reserved under International and Pan-American Copyright Conventions.
No part of this book may be reproduced in any manner whatsoever without written permission from the publisher, except in the case of brief quotations embodied in critical articles and reviews.

ACKNOWLEDGMENTS

Acknowledgment is made to the following publications for poems originally appearing in them:

Dash: "Scholar, Dementia Ward" (contest finalist)
Memoir (&): "Passing Bell for Kobun Chino, Sensei" (second prize)
Nimrod: "First Tuesdays at Hospice" (contest finalist)
Common Ground: "Visitor" (third prize)
Red Wheelbarrow: "The Good Word"

Publisher: Leah Maines

Editor: Christen Kincaid

Cover Art: "Falling Stars, Bristlecone Pine" by Irene Reti, 2014.
ireneretiphotography.smugmug.com

Author Photo: Julie Atkinson

Cover Design: Elizabeth Maines McCleavy

Printed in the USA on acid-free paper.
Order online: www.finishinglinepress.com
          also available on amazon.com

Author inquiries and mail orders:
Finishing Line Press
P. O. Box 1626
Georgetown, Kentucky 40324
U. S. A.

Table of Contents

Last Regrets 1

Angel Manor 2

Less 3

The Good Word 4

Assisted Living 5

Last Stop 6

Chocolate 7

Scholar, Dementia Ward 9

First Tuesdays at Hospice 10

Dreamer at the Helm 11

Passing Bell for Kobun Chino, Sensei 19

Still 20

Water-strider 21

Treasure 22

Vigil, Crestline Nursing 23

Long Valley 24

Red Fir's Counsel 25

Visitor 26

Death, ... 27

For Radha

Last Regrets

Pneumonia's deepened,
better come. I drop it all
    for a call like this.

        Numb flight. A brother's
bear-hug. *Staff says Dad's "resting."*
        Guestroom sheet's turned down.

        I'm so unready.
A gentle, forbearing man—
        we'll greet him at dawn.

Ringing shatters sleep.
Brother's knock—*Undertaker*
    at six . . . All alone.

        I would have entered
that room, stayed all night, his breath
    a puff on my cheek—

        would've stroked his hair,
forehead, knuckles—sent him off
        knowing. I would have.

Angel Manor
    Lynn

Here's the one you came to visit—fetal
curl in a recliner, spittle thread, chin
to knee. You're glad for time to face her
just before she wakes—oily hair pulled
back, sunken temples, bottomless silence.

Eyelids stutter open: her skittish, hungry
glance caroms off the walls, finds you,
steadies, clears, the way a waking infant
seeks a mother's face and fastens there—
spacious world shrunk to a tunnel of eyes.

What can you say that matters? Anything.
It's the tone that counts; a steady cadence
draws her in. Reach out slowly, stroke her
forehead first, the pointy shoulder, wrist.
Corners of her mouth twitch—
                                    a flickered
smile? Is she reaching? A finger tics.
Take her tremor, hold it, bone on bone,
pulse that shudders back and forth, shared
heartbeat. How long can you hold on?

Less
Michael

i.

Grips the bed-rail like a cliff-edge,
still can't roll onto his side
to let us slide the soiled pad out.
Lift him, and I'm holding bones.
Femur's stark, corded with tendons,
knee joint thicker than shaft. I could
circle his thigh with thumb and finger.
He's shaking with effort. *Can't—I can't!*

ii.

Now even my daily handshake,
coming and going—it's too much.
Barely awake when I slip in.
Snoring already, little whimpers
on the exhale—urgent scraps,
as if to settle things awry.
It stops—a pause that lengthens,
balloon that wants to waft him off.

iii.

Bathed and shaved, fed his ice cream
spoonful—chocolate. He's lucid, radiant.
Holds my outdoor hand in his, still
strong. He's slurry-voiced—*Ah waarm yu.*
Nothing but skeleton, skin and joy.
Bedroom clock's dicing things.
Singular crux of blood and hope,
time and bone, reduced to love.

The Good Word
  Bill

He's asleep on his side, knees up; near the end
  the body returns to its intimate curl. It's so
    quiet before I lay a hand on his shoulder
to rouse him, and have to shout to be heard.

The retort he must have used for 90 years—
  What's the Good Word? My part—"How you been?"
    Real good. He sleeps all day, can't stand up,
refuses food. *Real good.* A Navy man.

Every week I show up for the tales
  that anchor this stubborn life—the horse he rode
    to school, every ship he mustered on,
the battles, ports-of-call—always more.

I help him sit up, hipbones sharp in my palms.
  He's ninety-eight, wants to reach a hundred. "Why?"
    His head snaps up like he touched a cattle fence.
Dead's for a long, long time, my friend.

Will I find his pills? In the drawer—
  with cufflinks, tie-pin, key ring, Chinese coins,
    eye drops, stamps, tarnished Navy buckle,
glasses, dry pens, ointment, a plain gold ring.

Then one day he's gone. The bed is stripped.
  Like my father—just before I arrived.
    What's the Last Word, Bill? *Goodbye.*
Each one could be the last. So they say.

Assisted Living

I round the curve too fast: I'm almost on him—
man on his back at the edge of the road, with wheelchair,
mailbox hanging open, mail a halo in the mud.
Skid to a stop at his feet, hit the flashers,
leave the door ajar. An arm and leg—his left—
waving to right him, crablike; right side's inert.
Set up the wheelchair, lift beneath his arms:
I can't do it—till he pushes up with
the one good arm and leg, flops into the chair.
Shit!—what if he has broken bones?
Pick up the muddy mail, drop it in his lap.
He points to the box: sure enough, lodged in
the back, a package. Wheel him back to the home,
amazed how much his one leg helps. The gate
slams behind, the staff fusses around him: no
breaks, it seems. I turn to leave, he beckons me
close: "Fye, fo, tree, to, won—" counting on his hand.
A joke, I think: he's blasted off. When I reach
the gate, it's locked. Ah—the combination.

Last Stop
Robert

I lean in close to stroke his brow,
the silver wisps. He's mute now,
almost inert, head lolling.
Scans the room, glances up;
what's that old song on the radio?

When he was lucid and mobile, like brothers
we'd cruise the wharf, check out the swell.
Heard his kid-pranks—hubcaps lifted,
cops mooned, panties up a flagpole.
Later a brilliant teacher: students
flocked to him, fanned his fabled wit.

Sweet doo-wop tune that spun out
longing as we teens shuffled a gym floor,
clinging to someone, eyes shut.
I'll bet he was in the balcony, kissing,
hands where he'd dreamed they'd be.

Last stop, Marianne's—always strawberry.
That's where I saw the future: a cone
at first, then a cup, my spoon to his mouth,
then a drool. Like the mind—a jokester,
fumbled his punch-lines, later the set-up,
sentences frayed, ends left dangling.

The Drifters croon, *There goes my baby* . . .
We were wired for flare and jolt,
circuits snapping. That's what we knew
of how things end. Now, his gaze
on ceiling tiles, listening, maybe.

Chocolate
    Corey

Passes most days frozen now,
whole body a rictus in a recliner.
Tries to stop his slide to the floor:
the slightest tilt can kindle shame,
words caught deep in the throat.

Legs will not cooperate,
face a mask that looks like torment
and could be ecstasy, each phrase
a rune. Signals for *drink, more,*
stop. His thought obscure, beyond us.

Still, he'll lean into a walker,
stagger to the door, look up with hope.
Locked. He needs to be turned around,
guided back, a hand on his belt—
as if I could spare him another fall.

Pants down, he needs to piss
but doesn't trust the toilet's behind him.
Stands helpless, lets a stream go
on the wall, his feet. *S-s-sorry.*
"It's o.k., o.k." A moment's brotherhood.

A towel to wipe him and the floor;
totter together toward his bed,
feel him sway and down we go.
I break his fall but see the fear in his
glance: betrayed? He slackens—guffaws!

Whatever cheer he's summoned wanes,
gaze inward, a house of drawn shades . . .
then leans into the touch he's shunned—
an arm stroked, eyelids kissed—
disarms us both when words dry up.

Slack now, gold crowns glinting. Bedside,
a bonsai-ed Christmas tree; a model dory:
"Granddad's Dreamboat"; advent calendar—
"24 Days of Joy." Dark chocolate
waits beneath each shuttered date.

Scholar, Dementia Ward

Hefts the tome—it's dense.
Lifts a cover, leafs pages,
fingers a line: deep
silence. Nods. Snaps the book shut.
It's been upside down.

First Tuesdays at Hospice

The reading's slow, each name
        a ripple that laps at silence.
                We hear those we tended—
squeeze of a flung-out hand.

Startle at the name of a once-close
        friend—our age, vital,
                at our children's births.
        How could it have happened?

Most names we don't know.
        Here the mind sideslips:
                it can't hold so much loss,
all that ardor quenched.

Night-air's chill, breath shallow.
        One life seems enough
                to lose—but this tsunami,
name after name after name.

Dreamer at the Helm
Doug

> When you look for God,
> God is in the look of your eyes,
> nearer to you than yourself.
> —Rumi

i. taste it

Short sunburnt man, a crushing handshake,
soft-spoken Apollo—could have been a son
and asked to be a brother—global sailor I envied
for living his dream. Now a tumor on his brain.
"A little one," he says. "Gotta be zapped."

A year from now we'll lounge on teak
above a virescent cove in Rarotonga.
Or I'll visit where his meals are wheeled in.
Or lean from the stern of a sloop not his,
watch his ash garnish the wake.

My mother said it—*just a blip*; in a year she
passed through animal, vegetable, mineral.
So I fix a simple meal—dice beets, turnips,
cabbage for a friend who still can taste it—
trying not to know what I know.

ii. Doe Bay

You can go a thousand miles and still not
reach the present. Land erupts from ocean
here, black rock forms a necklace—glitter-line
between the tides. I'm here, but I'm not *here*.

So a raven's approach across the water helps,
rowing on damp air, passing near enough to hear
a wash of wings, a creak, to feel in the shoulders
what it's like—long pulls, slate gulf beneath.

Radiate first—burn a little more each week.
Small things done steadily. Tug's hauled a barge
out the Strait of Juan de Fuca, scarcely crawling—
and now it's just a mite on the horizon.

Raven's gone. What I want—not salt water's
purl on gravel, firs crowding shore. This:
kayak up the Strait, blades winking sun,
him doing what he loves, on water. Here.

iii. sleep

All night, the mockingbird; unfinished dreams.
October's conflation—jasmine and woodsmoke.
Now children at play.
                        I don't want to call,
don't want to see him shrunk to a knot, mostly
silent, unable to dress. I saw it with my mother—
the perimeter a noose, a shrinking ring of light.

My neighbor throws lumber around his yard,
flings it from pile to pile as if it were to blame.
The Raiders must have lost. *The unexamined life.*

Doug's been facing the truth for months.
What would I want in his place? Touch,
everyday warmth, voices I know beside me.

Chainsaw, car horn, low-flying plane—
what it takes to drag me from sleep.
Any place but there. O.K., I'll call. I'll go.

iv. language

He's leaning forward in his chair, too close
to the small TV—a daytime game show,
spangled couples that cheat and tell.
Looks up when I step in, turns away.

How to find one true thing to say . . .
You look O.K. . . . No. I've missed you.
Wears a diaper. She has him stand to change.
He turns away to hide a shriveled cock.

She's on break. He's down to single words,
waves fiercely at her shrinking car,
eyes filled, mouth shaking, the tumor
a dam that weeps at every fissure.

He wants to walk—arm-in-arm, our fingers
interlaced, along the drive. From leaves
he scuffs a roundish pebble. Now and then he'll
squeeze my hand, tag of a mute monologue.

Kicks the stone and waits for me to tap it—
diagonals up the drive, a micro-soccer game
past lizard-scuttle, sticky monkey-flower.
Reduced to the language of a shared pebble.

I look up—the great Pacific! Abstract for him.
The game is real, the stone that skitters;
he waits till I retrieve and drop it at his feet,
looks up and kisses me full on the mouth.

v. soup

Potatoes, crisp and milky, carrot rounds
that roll away, the kettle's chatter.

Sweet smack of garlic, pale onions,
a towel for the eyes, even at peace.

It's a matter of taking *this*, and *this*,
content with what comes to hand.

I've made it before, but not for him,
and not for itself—one item at a time.

He gave me the sea; now he sits and
rocks—my words, his nods—picks at lint.

Tarragon, oregano, salt. And the one
ingredient I'll never confess: ketchup.

Didn't think I'd love to cook this late,
this quiet, windows black and sweating.

Traffic's thinned, the season's first owl.
Let it simmer; no one's hungry now.

vi. dead weight

There, through the window, sliding from his
chair—can't walk now; can barely cross
his legs or rub his nose. I want to leave, but
kneel at his feet: the eyes flicker—he *knows*.

He wants so little—looks in my eyes to find me.
I brush his cheek; he kisses back—loud smack—
and rolls away. Lift him under the arms—
*dead weigh*t it's called—to the bed, head lolling.

He was gorgeous, like anyone once, invincible.
He'll vomit on the quilt. Towels to wipe him;
lift him out—clean sheets—and back. He'll
look up, contrite, regarding, then glaze over.

*Let there be a place I don't need to stroke
his ruined face—where, hands on the wheel,
he reads its thrum, squints up at tell-tales, guides
a glistening hull through the strait's rip-tide.*

That's a prayer out the window. *Let us be
anywhere but here.* That's another.

vii. open

He thrashed, kicked down the sheet, knees splayed.
I put down *Charlotte's Web*: too meandering.
Tried Rilke: he clawed the bed-rail. Rumi then:
> *God's joy moves from unmarked box to unmarked box,*
> *from cell to cell. As rainwater, down to flowerbed.*
> *As roses, up from ground . . .*

The words had weight that settled on his chest
and slowed his churning. He breathed from the belly.
Fern and ficus stirred in the window breeze.
> *Now it looks like a plate of rice and fish,*
> *now a cliff covered with vines,*
> *now a horse being saddled . . . .*

Simple words—drops on a tongue
in the wind. He traced wrinkles on the sheet,
careful patterns I couldn't see, then stopped.
> *It hides within these,*
> *till one day it cracks them open.*

He looked up. I saw the year's waste—
contorted, channeled mask—and the eyes
of the man I knew, serene now, lucent.

Who am I to talk about *God's joy* for him?
Leave it this way: he always gave me more
than the little I brought him, weeks apart.

Out the high window, gulls were wheeling;
he knew that meant rain. I should have, too,
hands cupping his cheeks. Cracked open.

viii. terms

Halyard, forestay, spreader, shroud—
he loved the terms. Block and cleat,
clew and leach, tell-tale, batten, luff—
he loved precision, brevity.

> *It could have been worse. A jibe*
> *and the boom clipped my head,*
> *slammed me into the cockpit.*
> Haul-in the mainsheet! *Dazed,*
> *I heard him and couldn't understand.*

Each line braided with a color
its own: mainsail, outhaul, spinnaker,
jib—red, yellow, green, blue.
Language he loved—and risk.

> *Off one rail, last sun on the fogbank;*
> *off the other, a near-full moon;*
> *above, white sail, black mast;*
> *down here, gray deck—all beautiful.*

He should be here still: offshore breeze,
warm and ragged, not quite dangerous
but strong enough to wake a dreamer
at the helm. Chop tattoos the hull.

> *How I sat on the gunwale—an inch or two—*
> *it could've been my temple. Dead at that speed.*
> Next time, *he said,* you'll know.

I heel, close-hauled, beat to windward.
Headwind thrums the stays, scours the mind,
gives the body something else to do.
Just not enough. Not nearly.

Passing Bell for Kobun Chino, Sensei
—We're separate from nothing.

In that moment of knowing—beside the lake,
        your daughter gone under—surely, no thought
                but to follow, and the body's faith that it can.
        And then? Did you swim down to twilight,

paw toward weeds beyond your reach, exhale,
        believing another stroke would find her?
                Did you touch, knowing neither could rise,
        draw her close as you settled down deeper?

Prophet who didn't believe; you *knew*.
        The planet yields so few—and so casually
                takes you away. A vacancy I didn't feel until
        you weren't here to fill it. A final parent lost.

                *

Tell me what breathed you breathes us all.
        Tell me we can live, eyes open, and know
                this touch is the last. Let me be a membrane
        to caress what comes, and let it pass through.

Wind chime. Scrub jay. Sun through fog.
        Not ideas, not words; the things themselves.
                We say hello a thousand times and
        never fully mean it. Or goodbye.

The gulf between absence and presence
        is tiny, profound. I spent decades
                inching over it, clinging to your hand.
        So what if they waver—the first steps alone.

Still

Maurice

Hates that I follow his Haitian lilt
so poorly, make him repeat, detests
that I take his elbow after his bird-like
frame crumples and I hoist him up.
Pushes me off, as if soiled by touch.

Seems there's always a roommate's TV,
volume cranked to rattle the bed rails.
Hard-breathing soldiers ambush a dragon
that scorched a battalion—a single pass.

Sit at the bed, hands to myself. He's
moaning, eyes squinched, clawing air.
His hand drops to my lap. Unthinking,
I cradle its cool in mine . . . A stillness
spreads, palm to arm to breath.

The P.A. calls for Doctor Blank,
cry down the hall, a siren shrinks,
the dragon groans its last, a nurse
chatters in, stops, backs out . . . quiet.

. . . Lift my head—dusk already—
lay his warmed hand on his chest;
he's asleep. Next day, an empty bed.

Water-strider
    for Daryl

i.

Near midnight, shuffling to the toilet,
   the body teeters, pitches face-first
      to the floor. You can move: no breaks.
         You can call them. Family stumbles out,
            turns a harsh light on and, crooning, hoists
            up beneath the arms, guides you forward.
        Something's changed: you're outside your body,
     watch it stagger with you trapped inside.
   It tugs you along like the old ranch dog
that kept you close, nudging at your knees.

ii.

After the storm you want to visit Westcliff,
   check the swell—double-overheads
      stacked up in the lane, crawling with surfers,
         water-striders creeping toward the break.
            "I told 'em, keep me free o' pain—
            'induced coma' till I slip away—like
        that guy: rode it all the way. Now he's
     settled; he's sinking. I wanna go like that."
    With every full-on wave the cliff shakes.
"I love this place.   I   love   it."

Treasure
> *Don*

Wednesday night he fell asleep and didn't
    wake on Thursday. Or did he? In fear? Joy?
        Fragrance of late jasmine? . . . She heard nothing.

What he carried: triple by-pass, now
    a faulty valve. It made him sweeter, lighter,
        more curious than ever—irrepressible.

When did we see him last? September maybe,
    lunch with friends and his brother who toils daily
        at rowing and tennis, fleeing his own sentence.

The Greek Festival, rosemary spice of gyros,
    sizzled kebabs, crunch of sycamore leaves.
        He bought lemon sherbet, passed it around.

We conjure that day—Don in his wide-brimmed, floppy
    hat, sweater tied at his waist, sunglasses
        sliding down the nose, quizzing vendors,

What's your treasure here? Wooden flutes,
    hand-made sweaters, baklava, of course—his
        delight that someone made them for delight.

He knew it begins as loss, and ends in full
    surrender. We vow to follow that floppy hat,
        savor the sherbet weeping on our hands.

Vigil, Crestline Nursing
Marian

Arrive for the last of her brothers' feud—
        hard words, a stomp from the room—
                and step into the hush an ignorant man.

Pull a steel chair up to the bed:
        lank hair, skin chalky, breath jagged,
                eyes wide toward the sealed window.

She's someone's sister, someone's love.
        Rinse the cloth, fold it on her
                damp brow, tell her you'll stay.

Hum that nameless fragment, stroke
        her forearm, turn the warming cloth.
                Notice the breath has slowed and slackened,

face dusky, eyes focused,
        inquiring, on a point above your head.
                The pauses lengthen, as if she'd just

forgotten to breathe, until there's a sigh
        that nothing follows. Stand and enter
                the space her still-clear eyes are fixed on.

Seventy years someone lived
        within, behind those hungry eyes.
                Tips of the fingers have started to blue.

Pines pitch in the wind, limbs
        lush, exuberant . . . What did she see?
                Close and hold her lids, for the brothers.

Long Valley
Dan

We watch his favorite rope operas,
reruns—"Gunsmoke," "Ponderosa."
Over hoof-beats, spills his story:
totaled his bike, straggled to ER—
brain tumor. He knew what it meant.

Swears he's not a smoker. Hides them
in every drawer, in secret pockets.
Visits the smoking court on the hour,
lights up, forgets, drops ash in his lap
that burns holes in his plaid pajamas.

Doesn't rouse to my knock today—
sleeping through "The Long Valley"?
No, he's upright, slumped and sweaty,
shivering—hands like aspen leaves
in storm; his thick frame quakes the bed.

Looks straight at me: "Kiss me. Kiss me!"
His skull slick, brow salty,
harsh cheek—over and over
till the shaking drops him, last wakeful
moment. Knew just what he wanted.

Red Fir's Counsel
Yuba Pass

To stand in witness while others come
and go—for centuries—it's what we do.
A blizzard beheads us? Room for another.

You, too, witness your kind: hold them,
hear their rattles, shut their eyes,
inch toward the one stone Fact.

And still you lull yourself: you tamp
your panic at their shudders and silence,
lean toward the dying—and cling to the light.

What you want lives inside fear.
When wildfire escalades, stand
and let it pass through you—
                              know
the smoke of your own dying. You'll be
nurse log for a thousand seeds.

Visitor

Carol

At first I'd step into that room, eyes
down, braced as if something were
coiled beneath her bed. But she would
without fail slide her mottled
arm of bone from under sheets
to find my hand. I'd fold her claw—
still warm—in both my mitts and hold it
till I felt her flutter-pulse;
then I'd start to breathe again.

One day I smelled what huddled under
that bed: my poorest frightened self.
I lifted it, shaking, almost weightless,
into my lap and stroked its cool—
There now, dying looks like this.
Today I'm at her shoulder, to follow
the jagged breaths where they go,
surprised—not that I can love her,
but that I might love myself.

Death,

you took the parents I longed to settle with
while I dragged my bag of slights: couldn't
my father say *I love you* once in sixty years?
Until I learned he was himself an error:

teen parents hustled to give him away.
Until I learned he missed my whole first year
hunting Axis subs off an African coast while
Mother clutched me, desperate for a bit of him.

I understand at last you sink us all,
but here's the solace you cloaked in loss:
a beat and its echo, here, in the heart's
squeeze, 80,000 times a day;

in breath that enters and leaves on its own;
in tenderness for children that forgives the rest.
I still can't praise your iron erasures
but hold me this close awhile—no closer.

Charles Atkinson's first poetry collection, *The Only Cure I Know* (San Diego Poets Press), received the American Book Series award for poetry; a chapbook, *The Best of Us on Fire*, won the Wayland Press competition. A third volume, *Because We Are Men*, was awarded the Sow's Ear Poetry Chapbook Prize. His most recent full-length collections are *Fossil Honey*, from Hummingbird Press, and *World News, Local Weather*, a prizewinner from Finishing Line Press. He has also received the Stanford Prize, the *Comstock Review* Prize, the Paumanok Poetry Award (SUNY Farmingdale), the Emily Dickinson Award (Universities West Press), *The Ledge* Poetry Prize, *The Sow's Ear* Poetry Prize, and Garrison Keillor's Poems of Gratitude prize.

He taught writing of various sorts for 30 years at the University of California, Santa Cruz, and still resides near Santa Cruz with his wife—writer and artist Sarah Rabkin.

www.ingramcontent.com/pod-product-compliance
Lightning Source LLC
LaVergne TN
LVHW041513070426
835507LV00012B/1539